Daddy's Girl

A Daughter's Tribute

Understanding the Value of Resiliency

Edited by Sherri Matthews

Cover Design: Fabrienne Alexander

Author Photo: Captur3 The Light Photography

ISBN: 978-0-578-92664-3

We hope you enjoy this book from Moving Forward Together Initiatives, LLC. For more information, you may visit
https://movingforwardtogetherinitiativesllc.com

Preface

To your surprise, I did not think about writing this book. I was actually working on another manuscript. But someone very special, a fierce woman of God contacted me one day and told me that I needed to write a book about my relationship that I had with my father, "Daddy." It was a week after we had my dad's home going service. I said to myself, a book about my father? She informed me that this would be therapeutic for me and for others. I have to admit I was a little hesitant. I thought to myself: *"How would I get started? Can I really write my thoughts out on paper? Who would read it? I do not know a thing about publishing."* I was optimistic. I started to search for workshops about self-publishing, attended multiple webinars, prayed, and grabbed my laptop and started typing away.

Whether I was typing at my parents' home, in my car, or outside, I would reminisce about the good, bad, and sweet memories that I had with my "Daddy." This journey has been tough but each day I strive to be a better me, thinking of the memories of my dad.

There are so many memories, however this book only touches on some of them, but describes a few of the struggles, victories, and many testimonies that my father faced throughout his life. I described my Daddy as being two cats and a tiger because he had more than nine lives. When doctors said he would not make it, God said He was not through with him yet.

You may be reading this book and are currently coping with the loss of a loved one, or you may be dealing with some challenges in your life. Don't give up. Hold on. Encourage yourself. You got this! It is my hope that as you read this book, take your time to review the reflections, and be intentional in completing the *"Call for Action."* Make a vow to yourself to live your life on purpose.

Table of Content

Dedication

I dedicate this book to my Daddy, hero, soldier, friend, cheerleader, and number one supporter. You fought the good fight. Well done, thy good and faithful servant.
I will always love you, miss you, and hold your memories close to my heart.
It is your presence and love that will forever live on.

Wayne F. Nelson
(Oct 17, 1949 - November 3, 2020)

Love
Daddy's Girl

ACKNOWLEDGEMENTS

Change happens when you have people that mentor, lead, guide, and encourage others to be the best version of themselves. Thank you to all of the mentors that see the value in others when at times they do not see in themselves. None of this would have been possible without my awesome village of family and friends that guided and supported me along this journey of completion. I will forever be grateful for the love, prayers, and support that you have provided my family and I during the process of my dad's transitioning and as I discover a new normal without my dad physically here.

I would like to thank my mother for the sacrifices that you made throughout your life for our family. For the care that you provided Daddy until the very end. Thank you.

To my sisters; Dina, Monique, Keyia, and Keysha, we may not always agree, but know that I love you and pray for the best for each of you.

To my sister-friends (you know who you are), thank you for being there through the ups and downs in this journey called life.

To my prayer warriors, I do not have the words to express how much your prayers are appreciated, have touched my heart, and pressed me to continue to live life to the fullest.

To my creative cover designer, Fabrienne Alexander, thank you for making my vision come to life.

To my amazing editor, Sherri Matthews, thank you for your time and feedback.

Most of all, I would like to thank God, without God, none of this would have been possible. He has given me peace and strength throughout this journey. It is through Him, that all things are possible.

Yolanda M. Nelson

The Beginning

"You are the sum total of everything you've ever seen, heard, eaten, smelled, been told, forgot — it's all there. Everything influences each of us, and because of that, I try to make sure that my experiences are positive."
Maya Angelou

The Beginning, I would have to start with how my mom and dad (Linda and Wayne) met. The story has it that they met at Sid Booker Highline. My mom was sitting at the bar with her girlfriend, Carrie. Larry, my dad's friend, started to speak with my mom and my dad started to have a conversation with Carrie. The ladies decided to use the bathroom and talked about it, and that is when they decided to switch. Carrie exchanged phone numbers with Larry. And my mom exchanged phone numbers with my dad. They began chatting on the phone; Daddy would finally take Mommy to her job then hang out. After six months of dating, my dad proposed on my mom's birthday. And that is how it all started!

June 23, 1973, was when my parents decided to make that commitment in front of God, family, and friends. My parents would describe this as a day to remember.

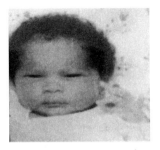

On October 9, 1978, I was born in Philadelphia, PA, to Linda and Wayne Nelson. It happened to be a surprise. When my mother went to go for her check-up after having my twin sisters (we are only 13.5 months apart), she learned that she was pregnant with me. From the union of my mom and dad, I am #4, *"the baby."* We lived in Philadelphia, PA until, I was three years of age, and then my parents decided to move to New Jersey for a safer environment and more opportunities. As a child, I looked to my dad as my *hero, soldier, funny guy, Vietnam Veteran, Purple Heart recipient, and the life of the party.*

At the age of six, I can remember Daddy coming to pick me up from Kindergarten, I saw him and ran into his arms. I felt on top of the world. It was at that moment I felt like I was ***Daddy's Girl***.

My father enlisted in the United States Marine Corps in 1967. In the Marine Corps, Daddy was an Infantry Machine Gunner. While fighting for his country, daddy was wounded in combat (Vietnam War), in

Kindergarten Picture

which he earned a Purple Heart. After coming from the War, Daddy became dependent on alcohol. I believe that his alcohol dependency was possibly related to Post Traumatic Stress Disorder (PTSD). During the time of his alcoholism, it changed the person he was. He became abusive to my mother. It was scary at times. On occasion, we wondered *how the bills would get paid. Would we be safe*? My mother decided that it was best to leave so that we could be in a stable environment. That was a difficult time in my life to witness. We received public assistance, which helped with groceries and bills. It was frightening at times, and there were some moments in which we didn't know how we would make it. Now the separation between my mom and dad, moving in and out, and coming back happened more than once. But God!

I knew that my dad loved his family dearly throughout my early childhood years, but dealt with addiction. That was his struggle. Through prayer, support of family and friends, things were going to change. They had to change. Within time, daddy received help that he needed, went to Alcoholics Anonymous (AA), became involved in church, and we were back together again as a family.

Daddy worked at the Philadelphia Naval Shipyard as a carpenter for years until its closing. He took pride in working at the shipyard. I wonder, was it because he was close to his love, the water? As a child, I anticipated him coming home from work. He would always come into the house cheerful, with a smile on his face, and with candy!

When everyone was together, the weekends at my parent's home were memorable. Saturday mornings would include completing our assigned chores (usually dusting the furniture in the living room, dining room, and family room). We didn't have a lot of money, but my parents would treat us to McDonald's breakfast on Saturday mornings, Daddy would get up and make a pot of Cream of Wheat or home fries. Daddy didn't cook much (besides fish), but when he did, it was great. Rumor is that he taught my mother how to cook when they first got married.

I enjoyed my Saturday afternoons because they were mainly spent outdoors. We would ride our bicycles outside until it got dark, play jump rope, listen to music, and play in the dirt. The street that we lived on consisted of kids that were the same age as my sisters and me. To this day, some of the same neighbors on the street look out for each other.

Summertime was spent at my grandmothers'

homes in Philadelphia. My twin sisters would go to my Dad's mother's house, and my oldest sister and I would go to my mom's mother's home. We would alternate the summers. I enjoyed spending time with my grandmothers, and I do believe that they enjoyed having my sisters and I. Some fond memories were waking up in the morning at my dad's mother's home (we called her Mom) and making breakfast. She would make us all drink half a cup of prune juice with our meal. At first I could not stand the taste of prune juice but as I got older I realized it was not too bad. We would sit at the table once breakfast was ready, pray, and make a toast. We would grab our prune juice and say '*Toast to the Nelson girls. Weeeeeeee....*'" Talk about good times.

My mother's mom, known as Granny, was quiet and stern. But I learned how to break her hard shell. I would laugh as well as joke around with her. Sometimes I would get a smile. She loved to bake and would make the best blueberry pie. I wish I could bake like her. During my teenage years, Granny passed away of cancer when I was thirteen- years old.

As for me as a child, I felt different. I knew there was something unique about me, something inside of me that would be birthed out eventually. I just had to discover what that was. In school, I strived to be the best and excel. I wanted to make mommy and daddy proud. I was self-motivated, felt learning was fun, and was a high achiever. I was accepted into a college-bound program in the eighth grade, which opened my eyes to learning about college and various careers. I enjoyed learning so much at that point. I knew college was for me.

During my childhood years, my dad loved to go fishing and enjoyed being on the water. I can see why, when I look at the water now, as for me, it represents tranquility, peace, freedom, and God's beauty. I believe that fishing was a source of therapy for himself. A time that he could breathe, reflect, enjoy God's creation, and have a good time with his buddies. Daddy would wake up early on Saturday mornings (around 3:00am) and meet up with his homies to get on the charter boat to fish all day. Daddy would catch sea bass, whiting, flounder, and halibut. His famous saying was, *"You Got to Hook*

'Em to Cook 'Em. "

A lot of times, he would win a prize for catching the largest fish and had been noted in the newspaper quite often. He was so proud to be a sports fisherman. Afterward, he would come home, fillet the fish, and fry it up. Talk

1991-Daddy giving me a lesson on how to filet fish.

about delicious! He kept a separate freezer just for his filleted fish. I never learned to filleted nor cook fish, because I could always count on daddy!

My aunt told me that he developed his love for fishing as a child. As a child, daddy would visit his relatives in Tappahannock, Virginia. He would fish with his uncles and cousins. It was something that he enjoyed and he loved the reward of catching a fish. With time, he was known as Wayne, "the fisherman."

If he was not fishing, you would find my dad playing the game of chess, listening to jazz, or chatting with his friends. But don't forget his love for Cadillacs. My dad owned many Cadillacs and I can remember one of his favorites was a 1978 blue and white Cadillac Coupe Deville. My sisters and I thought his Cadillac looked like a boat but my dad loved and took pride in it. He had a love for life, a people person, and was always smooth with his nice suits when it was time to go out. Whether going to church, celebrating his birthday, or attending an event, daddy was always sharp as a tack. He had one of the bedrooms remodeled to have a walk-in closet for his suits and Stacey Adam shoes. I can still smell his aftershave, Royal Copenhagen, or the fragrance of his oil, Egyptian Musk. Those smells remind me of the earth, a cool breeze, and peace. Oh, the memories.

Reflection: Not until reflecting on my life did I realize how much the early part of my years, my beginning, has played such an intricate role in creating the person I am today. From the good, bad, scary, and okay moments, God has been there every step of the way. As I am writing this, I realize one thing. My dad was an over comer. He did not allow his past trauma of being in the Vietnam War, which he witnessed, overtake him. He was victorious. Yes, he may have had his struggles, but he did not allow those struggles to overtake his life. Instead, Daddy became active in the Veterans of Foreign Wars (VFW).

Call for Action: Think about a young memory of your life. What if you could talk to your teenage self, the one thing you would say would be?

Youthfulness

"Good habits formed at youth make all the difference." Aristotle

My teenage years' experiences played a role in shaping/molding the person that I am today. Throughout my childhood, my parents bickered a lot. It came to a point where my parents just could not agree to disagree. My dad moved out and decided it was time to separate. My parents decided that one of my sisters and I would move in with my father. I was sixteen and in the 10th grade. I lived with my dad until I graduated high school. It was during this time that my relationship with my mother became strained. We would argue, and at that time in my life, it created a distance between us. I worked two jobs throughout those two years with my dad, went to school, purchased a car, and saved money.

My dad gave me a curfew, it taught me to be more responsible. But I have to admit, sometimes I did not make that curfew, and he would put the second lock on the door. Then he would have to answer the door when I came home. My dad started to decrease my curfew down by half an hour every time I was late. It went all the way down to 9:30 pm, and I finally learned my lesson! Living with my dad also meant that this was the first time I had to cook so I played around with ingredients. I thought I knew something in the kitchen, but honestly, I did not learn how to cook well until I reached my twenties.

While living with my dad, I was even more determined to apply to college and have a career. It was either February or March of 1997; I received an acceptance letter from Trenton State College, now known as The College of New Jersey. The sky was the limit, and nothing was going to stop me from attaining my dreams. I can remember my dad dropping me off to college. I felt grown, and I was on my own. I was on top of the world! So I thought. In that period of preparing to go to college and leaving, my mom and dad decided to try again, so they got back together. I disagreed with my parents trying again; I have to admit I was angry at first. But God knew best and had something else in mind. Thankful that God's thoughts and plans are greater than our own.

College was a whole new world for me. I started as a Pre-Med major. Wow! Did I struggle in my first year! I was not used to the rigorous coursework. I was used to getting straight A's without doing much studying during my high school years. I honestly had to work on my studying strategies, time management, and improving critical thinking skills. It got so bad that I ended up on academic probation my first semester of college. I had to make some changes that had to occur fast. I never told my parents about my academic probation. I was ashamed. Everyone looked upon me as the smart one. I just worked harder, signed up for tutoring services, and was off of academic probation the next semester. I began to understand, study differently, and excel.

When reflecting on college, this represented a time that I set forth to begin the journey of discovering myself. During my first year of college, I heard about nursing and all of the opportunities it would bring. At the end of my first year, I decided to change my major to nursing. While my first year was difficult, the nursing major was even more challenging. Far more than what I ever expected. The undergraduate program was considerably challenging, especially learning study skills/habits and time management was essential tools for an undergraduate student. I found myself questioning whether I was good enough, smart enough, and doubted if I could complete the nursing program. Some of my fellow African-American classmates experienced those same feelings and later changed their majors.

Throughout my college experience, my drive to succeed grew stronger. I had to make it. I had to graduate and become a registered nurse. I did not comprehend how important this would be in my adult life, but I just knew I had to accomplish this goal. And I understand why. A patient's life could be in your hands. You may be the first person to recognize a change in the patient's status; you may pick up something that isn't right and advocate for the patient. You may also be the person that helps to educate a patient, which equates to better patient outcomes. Or you could be the person who holds your patient's hand while they transition and take their final breath. I will never regret that decision I made and am grateful that being a nurse has helped me advocate for my parents, especially my dad.

With God as the source of my strength, after five years, I graduated. I can distinctly remember that day because my dad was right there supporting me. He was incredibly proud. As the baby of the family, I was the first to graduate from a four-year college/university. And not only did I graduate but I had landed my first job as a staff nurse on an Orthopedic Unit in New Jersey. I was always a planner (I think I get that from my dad since he was a Marine). Prior to graduation, one of the final nursing courses that I enrolled in was Leadership. One of the requirements was that the nursing students had to shadow three different leaders in nursing. I decided to find a leader at this particular hospital which was my number one pick to work upon graduation. Well, I made it happen. I can remember it clearly. It was February of 2002. I looked professional, had copies of my resume, and asked the right questions throughout my shadow/observation time. Talk about timing. By the end of that day, the hospital offered me a graduate nurse position! That following week, I received a letter in the mail congratulating me. Can you believe it?! I never interviewed for my first job! Talk about favor walks on two feet.

I didn't know what was to come and the importance and value of God's timing.

Daddy's hair was his trademark! The box (high fade)! I never knew why he liked it so much... lol!

Reflection: When considering this time in my life, what comes to mind is freedom and independence. From being allowed a curfew as a teenager than going on to college and living in a dorm. This was a time I began to feel like I was transitioning into adulthood with responsibilities. My faith in God kept me grounded during my time of transitioning into adulthood. And it was my dreams and goals in life that motivated me to keep moving forward.

Call for Action: Questions to consider:
1. What motivates you?
2. How are you showing up in the world?
3. What keeps you grounded?

New Beginnings

"Nothing can stop the power of a committed and determined people to make a difference in our society. Why? Because human beings are the most dynamic link to the divine on this planet." John Lewis

Once graduating college, I landed my first job and I got approved for my very first apartment on my own. It was an exciting time. I began working as a staff nurse on an Orthopedic Unit at a hospital in central New Jersey. That job was the start of my nursing career. I enjoyed working with the nurses, and I learned so much. I treated that unit like my second family. We were a dedicated team. At the start of my nursing career, I encountered racism, patient's family members who did not want me to touch them because of my skin color.

My nursing peers and the nurse manager stood by my side; valued me as a nurse, as a person. I will forever be grateful for my first nursing job! Within a year of nursing, my nurse manager said that she saw something in me, and I began to precept and orient nurses on the unit.

I could not believe that she asked me to take on this leadership role, being that I was a fairly new nurse. I studied all of the time, reviewed procedures, researched medications, and so forth. I wanted to be knowledgeable and the best at what I was doing.

After working 2.5 years on the orthopedic unit, I decided to apply to the OBGYN outpatient office at the same hospital. They hired me! In my role, I educated expectant mothers regarding nutrition and prenatal care, assisted the physicians in procedures, and collected some subjective and objective data from patients for the physicians. Those moments confirmed my love for teaching. I loved teaching the patients and reviewing something new with staff.

My mom and I began to work on our relationship but we had our ups and downs. What I can say is that when it came time to make medical decisions or anything that may affect my parents, my mom and dad relied on me for some advice. By them depending on my expertise, this made me feel special. During this time, my family learned that my dad was going into End Stage Renal Disease (ESRD) and had liver failure and needed to be on the transplant list. I can remember so vividly, I was visiting my parents' home, and daddy wanted to go for a walk. So that is what he did. Ten minutes had passed and he still had not returned. My sister and I went looking for him, walked down the street, got in our cars but could not find Daddy. Then we made some phone calls, went to the police station and they began to search. Six hours later, my dad had been found in the back of someone's yard in a coma. He developed hepatic encephalopathy, which resulted in a coma. Hepatic Encephalopathy is a decline in brain function related to liver disease. He was transported to the hospital via ambulance and given 24 hours to live that day. Well, that is what the doctors said. That evening, we called my parent's pastor, friends, as well as family. They came, sang hymns, and prayed. Five days later, Daddy was off of life support and breathing on his own. He even sang one of the songs that we sang to him. But God!

The year 2002-2003 was a busy, stressful, terrifying time for my family and me. This period was filled with many hospitalizations for my dad, like being admitted into the Intensive Care Unit (ICU). Most of the time, he received a poor prognosis. As time progressed, my dad started on dialysis and would go in and out of the hospital for several medical problems such as pneumonia and congestive heart failure. I can remember one day, I went to my parent's home, shoveled the snow and cleared the walkway, then headed to work. When I got to work, my manager informed me that I needed to make a phone call. That was just one of the frightening calls in my life. Upon leaving the house, after I shoveled the snow, my dad had a heart attack and was on a ventilator; at that time, doctors then gave him 24 hours to live again. This news brought back memories from the last time that he was on the ventilator and given 24 hours to live. He did not look well, and that is when I whispered into his ear and said, "*It's ok to go*." But God was not through with him yet. There was more for my dad to do; he had to fulfill his purpose, encourage others and had to continue to be a walking, living testimony.

September 2003 will be the month and year that I hold very dear. That is when my dad (who was already in the hospital) received a double transplant (a kidney and liver). He had a new leaf on life. It was an extended stay in the ICU, recovery was slow, but I recall the day I picked up my dad and took him home. He wanted me to stop by the car wash. I remember him speaking with the car wash attendees and telling everyone, *"Look, I got a double transplant!"* He pulled up his shirt so everyone could see how well his surgical scars healed. He was so excited that he had another chance at life, and we were just as excited also. That October, we had a party for my dad and entitled it *New Beginnings.* We invited some of his closest family and friends, and it was a time that I will always recall, and this was just the start of the many celebrations that we did for Daddy.

Throughout the following years, my parents were able to travel more and see the world. They enjoyed cruising with my aunt and uncle. Some of the places cruised were *Cozumel, Puerto Rico, Bermuda, Jamaica, Belize, and Dominican Republic.* My parents enjoyed the shows and the excursions. Daddy loved the all-you-can-eat-buffets. Something that I did not care for, but he wanted to get his money worth! With his new leaf on life, Daddy continued fishing with his friends, playing chess, and being the most supportive dad. If there was an event, graduation, a dinner, daddy was there!

As my parents continued to enjoy life, I

started my journey on discovering my purpose in life and how nursing played a role in that. It was 2005; I decided to leave my job to start working at a practical nursing school. I will never forget my first teaching experience. What was supposed to be a two-hour lecture turned out to be a ten-minute lecture. I spoke so fast and ran through my notes and the power points. I was nervous! Despite that day, I knew that I had discovered my purpose. The following year, I was hired at another practical nursing school and eventually offered a clinical manager position. I assisted with hiring new staff, planning out clinical rotations for 500 students, helped with orientation, taught an NCLEX review, and filled in when the staff could not teach a class. I did a lot, and it was stressful at times. I decided that it was time for me to go back to school for my Master's Degree if I wanted to teach at a community college level (RN students). And that is what I did. I worked during the day and completed coursework at night. It was a tough 27 months to complete my Masters in Nursing Education, but I did it! After I graduated, I gave myself a small graduation party. And you know who was there front and center, daddy. All smiles! I knew he was proud!

During this time my mom and I began to work a little more on our relationship. We started to travel to different Caribbean destinations with my aunts (my mother's sisters). Some of the areas that we visited include *Mexico, Dominican Republic, and Aruba* (by far my favorite). We went back to the same resort in Aruba years later, and it was still the same, Beautiful! I truly enjoyed our time together traveling and just enjoying nature, the beach, good food, and fun. We were free. Those trips were also a time for me to unwind and relax. My love for being by the water grew. I think I get that from Daddy.

Once I completed my graduate degree, the sky was the limit; I knew what I wanted to do in my life professionally. I wanted to take the next step and teach students that desired to be registered nurses. That was and has been my desire, my passion. A diploma school in New Jersey hired me as a Full-Time faculty member. Can you believe it? Me? Little Ol' Yolanda!!! I have to admit; I was nervous. I thought to myself: "*Do you really know what you are doing? Do you possess the knowledge and confidence to assist students in building upon their critical thinking skills and succeed?*" I worked with a great team of faculty and staff.

Each day, each week, I grew as an educator. I got involved and wanted to learn as much as possible. In 2010, a faculty member informed me about a fellowship for minority nurses that wanted to know more about leadership. I filled out the application and was selected. I attended monthly workshops, and they were eye-opening. The workshops opened my eyes to even more possibilities.

As I knew teaching was my calling, was I living out my life's purpose professionally? I urge you to *not take for granted moments in your life that you do not understand the why and how.* The Dean at the diploma school that I worked at contacted an editor in California. She flew in to come to speak with the faculty individually and discussed our personal writing goals. My turn had come to meet the editor. The time I spent with her (I forgot her name) was life-changing. When I sat with her, she informed me that she felt something within me, and it had to deal with mentorship. She instructed me to purchase a devotional entitled *Jesus Calling* and read it each day.

She also instructed me to work on a book about mentorship. Isn't it amazing how someone can see a gift or talent within you before you even see it within yourself? I did not realize that my passion was not only teaching but increasing diversity within the profession of nursing. I decided that I needed to go back to school to receive my Doctorate. I believed that if I received my doctorate, this would open up more doors for me, I would be able to expand and fully walk in my purpose. I began school in 2011 at Rowan University to obtain a doctorate in Educational Leadership. During this time, a lot of other things occurred. Well, you may be wondering if I ever wrote the book on mentorship. I started on that book years ago, and I plan to finish it soon. I may not have finished the book, but you will learn how that planted seed has now been cultivated in the coming chapter.

Reflection: This time in my life truly represented a time of discovery, new beginnings, stepping out on faith despite my insecurities, and enjoying time with family and friends. It was a time to appreciate the moments and celebrate life. During this time, I developed stronger bonds, grew as an individual, and received confirmation on what I needed to do with my

Surprise Party for Daddy. My sisters and I thought we were Charlie's Angels. Look at the Old G. lololol!

life. Now it was time to walk in it fully. I always say: *"You gotta name it, claim it, believe it, receive it, and then go walk in it."*

Call for Action: What are you doing about the things that matter most in your life? If you had no limits or fears, what do you want to give yourself permission to do, discover, or make room for this year?

Time to Blossom

"You can only become truly accomplished at something you love. Don't make money your goal. Instead, pursue the things you love doing and then do them so well that people can't take their eyes off of you." Maya Angelou

During this time of my life, so many things occurred. Mommy and Daddy continued to live their best life. Cruise, attend church, and enjoy life. I remained focused on completing my doctorate to grant me more opportunities. While this was happening, the diploma school I worked for closed; I obtained a new job as a Clinical Nurse Educator at a hospital in New Jersey. I must admit, at first I was intimidated regarding this role, and that is because I had not been in the hospital for a few years (besides being a Clinical Adjunct for some Associate Degree Nursing Programs). But as I began to work on my assigned unit, got to know the staff and the physicians, I began to get comfortable in my role. This time hired as the Clinical Nurse Educator on the Medical-Surgical Dialysis Unit, and I developed a new policy for Peritoneal Dialysis Cycler.

I enjoyed making rounds on the patients, checking on them to make sure that they understood their plan of care. I would quiz patients' floors, leave notes to ask their physicians, and sometimes sit and/or pray with them if they needed me to do that. I can recall asking a patient's husband if I could pray with them. The patient was not doing well. I prayed for peace and comfort. Days later, the patient passed away. I was grateful I had that opportunity to be there for both the patient and her spouse.

I have to admit, some patients were nervous when they saw me, and that is because after I educated them regarding their medications or questions that they had, I would quiz them the next day. I can remember passing a patient's room one day and he yelled out of his room, "I'm not ready for my quiz," That made my heart smile. Those are the special moments that I will always remember and hold dear to my heart when I think about that job.

I do believe that there was a reason for me to be at that job. My motto is if I could touch one life, one individual, well, that is what matters the most. As a Clinical Nurse Educator, I was also an advocate for patients. Sometimes, I would discover that some patients, unfortunately, did not have the resources to afford their medications and which is why they became hospitalized. I would speak with the assigned social workers, look up resources, contact pharmacies, and so forth to assure that patients had what they needed and remained compliant.

It was stressful at times, and although I knew I was making a difference when I educated staff and most importantly, the patients, I knew deep down that that was not my calling. I was missing out on teaching. While I continued my journey for my Doctorate, I opened a bakery along with two business partners, all while working full-time. My plate was full... I mean, it was packed. While I worked at the bakery on Saturdays, my dad would stop by now and then to get something sweet. I enjoyed seeing his big smile and appreciated those moments.

When I look back at that period of my life, I realize that I made some decisions without fully thinking it all out. I did not pray to God for wisdom in the decisions that I made. While I rushed in some of my choices, I learned a lot at the same time. It was a demanding, trying, difficult time in my life. I was working two jobs, attending school, making sure family was okay, and providing care to my aunt, who was now on hospice due to her terminal cancer diagnosis. After my aunt's passing, "Aunt B," whom I was very close to, I realized that the bakery was not part of my purpose. The following month, we decided to close our doors. I eventually resigned from my job and began as a Clinical Adjunct at two different Schools of Nursing.

While the demand for work and school was a lot, at the same time, it was rewarding. I was walking in my purpose. I was even more determined to complete my doctoral studies. The dissertation process was brutal, but I made it through, and on December 18, 2015, I graduated! A year had gone by since my aunt had passed away. I know she would have been proud. You know she cheered me on, called to check on me frequently till the very end until she could not speak any more to make sure that I was completing my assignments. You know God always gives you what you need at the right time.

May 2016 was the ceremonious time of earning my doctoral degree. It marked the official moment that you could call me Dr. Nelson (boy, I love that). It symbolized blood, sweat, tears, and many nights of staying up working on papers. I can remember bringing chapters of my dissertation everywhere to read, review, revise, and for others to look over. Grateful for the people in my circle; I know I most likely drove some of them bananas. I knew that obtaining this degree would provide more opportunities for me, but I did not realize the potential of opportunities that this would be for others.

During my graduation ceremonies, Daddy was the person right there, proud with a smile. I can remember, after graduation, dancing with him with my regalia still on. At that moment, Daddy said: *"That's enough, Yogi."* (Yogi is my nickname) Lolol! Sometimes I can be over the top with excitement, and as Daddy got older, he became a little stern or tried to act like he was. That week I threw myself a graduation party. I couldn't wait on anyone: Shoot, all of this hard work that I just completed. Nothing could stop me. I felt on top of the world. That party was a day that will never be forgotten. Everyone had a great time, including Daddy. He sat back, ate, and enjoyed the festivities.

For my graduation gift, my parents gifted me with a five-day cruise to Cozumel, Mexico. January 2016, my parents and I traveled to Florida and departed on the cruise ship to Mexico. We had such an awesome time. From the food to the shows to spending time with my mom and dad, that will be a time that I will always remember. I know that they were both proud parents, and I considered this as a start for my mom and me to work on our relationship. Daddy enjoyed himself. We even took a small tour in the town, met some locals, and toured a tequila store. What I did not realize is that this would be Daddy's last cruise. I will forever cherish those moments of fun, laughter, getting on each other's nerves, and best of all, peace.

Reflection: This time of my life represented a time to blossom, a time of discovery, excitement, and sometimes anxiety for the unknown. I did not know then that I now know the importance of being still, taking a breath, and waiting on God. Some decisions were made abruptly. I can appreciate the value of saying **NO**. After all, no is a full sentence! No. When making a decision, it is ok to say no, and it is also ok to take a little time to pray, think about it, and ask for more time before making that decision.

Call for Action: While you are making plans keep in mind to set goals, there are decisions that you will also have to make. Decisions can be simple or complicated. Considering your personal and/or professional journey, what decisions do you need to make currently? Have you taken time to reflect?

The Transition

"Sometimes God brings times of transition to create transformation." Lynn Cowell

February 2018 is when my dad was diagnosed with colon cancer. Before his diagnosis, my dad had been bleeding while using the bathroom. My mother noticed that something was wrong when she saw blood in the toilet. She had my dad go to the emergency room at their local hospital; a CT scan was performed and showed something abnormal.

With his recent diagnosis, Daddy became weak and not strong enough to drive. His transplanted kidney also showed signs of failure, which meant that he had to start back on dialysis. So, I planned weekly mini road trips with my dad. We would go to Raul's Barber Shop if he needed his haircut. I would make sure that he got into the Barbershop safely with his walker and then sat in my car. For him, the Barbershop represented a time to talk about fishing, get any updates, and just gossip. That was his time with his buddies. Once he finished getting his haircut, we would leave to get a couple of crabs at a seafood spot called Blue Claw. Then we would pick up some goldfish from the pet store for his fish that ate them. Lastly, I would ask him if he needed anything else; we may go pick up a pretzel, a pizza or pick up some medication from his pharmacy. I think Daddy wholeheartedly enjoyed that. He appreciated getting some fresh air, going for a ride, and chatting away. I called my vehicle "the vent machine." That is, when he would get into my car, he would open up if something was bothering him, or he just talked about whatever came to his mind. While I am grateful for those times, those memories, I wish I had more of those days.

Over the next year, daddy was hospitalized numerous times with pneumonia, sepsis, and respiratory distress. I can remember August 2018, his admittance to the hospital; I visited him that day, and he was not doing well. The health care team decided to intubate him because he was in respiratory distress. My mother felt that she needed to be by my father's side. So she got on the bus (she does not drive and refuses to ride with anyone to Pennsylvania) and arrived there by 11 pm. She had called me to say that she was there safely and sitting at my dad's side. An hour later, my mom called me again and told me that it was over. This time, I thought it was for real. But God! Doctors, nurses did not give up and within minutes, they found a heartbeat. God still was not through with my dad yet.

That morning, looking at my father on the ventilator and all of the tubes, machines, and alarms on, it could be frightening, even traumatizing. Doctors could not explain what exactly happened and did not think that my dad would pull through it. Within days, Daddy was off the ventilator and the following week, he transferred to rehab. I would always say that Daddy is a *walking, breathing, living testimony*. I say he is two cats and a tiger (because he had more than nine lives).

October 2018 marked a special time in my life; I was turning 40 years old. Daddy was recently discharged from rehab. So, I was feeling great. I planned out my party at a banquet hall that included a saxophone player, a special dance, a DJ, and a spoken word that I would say as I walked in the room. It was a night to remember but most importantly, it was a memorable night with my family and friends. I can remember Daddy looking sharp as a tack. With his suit hat, don't forget the feather on the side of his hat (smile). Daddy told me that he did not have to get up to dance because I danced all night. He said that I made him tired, lolol!

Due to daddy's strong desire to be baptized, March 8, 2020, marked the day that symbolized his relationship to Christ and the personal testimony of his life. The following week, my parent's church closed due to the COVID-19 pandemic.

My parents spent the next few months doing their weekly routine. Daddy would go to dialysis, doctors' appointments, and I would pick him up to go to the barbershop and do our routine of grabbing something to  eat, going to the pet store, and take care of any other things that my dad needed.

September 23, 2020 was not a good day. Daddy received the results of his most recent CT scan. It showed that his colon cancer had returned and spread to his left lung. That day I contacted my dad and asked what he wanted to do...He told me he wanted to go for a ride. So I picked him up, and that is what we did, drove. At first, the ride was silent, but then Daddy began to open up about the new prognosis. Doctors gave him six months to 1 year to live without chemotherapy or 1 year to 3 years with chemotherapy. It was a hard decision to make. And I wanted daddy to make that decision for himself. No matter what, he knew that my family and I would be there for him. I told him that, as my dad, I would support him in any decision that he made. As the scripture goes, God's plans and thoughts are greater than our own.

The next month was difficult for my family, my dad began to not tolerate dialysis, and he did not have an appetite, so he started to have some weight loss. Daddy began to complain of back pain and some shortness of breath with exertion. The first week of October, daddy went to the Emergency Room; tests determined that he developed a Hemothorax, which could relate to his recent lung cancer diagnosis. He was treated for two weeks in the hospital for Hemothorax. Doctors contemplated whether or not to start chemotherapy. Instead, they made another decision to wait due to my dad's weakness and declining health. Prior to his hospitalization, my family and I had planned a weekend trip for my dad for his birthday, but plans changed. Daddy ended up in the hospital for his birthday, so we brought the birthday party to him. My mom, sisters, and I decided to get a hotel right next to the hospital. We brought daddy dinner, a cupcake, and some gifts. He did not eat much, but you could tell that he enjoyed individual time with the family.

Two weeks later, my dad came home from the hospital, and we decided that we did not want him to go to rehab but that we would care for him. From the previous hospitalization, he became weaker and could not walk. My family pulled together, and my sisters and I decided that we would do around-the-clock care so that my mother would not feel overwhelmed. My sisters also took some time to have weekly bonfires outside to unwind and to do a weekly checkup. I really enjoyed that time.

This involved spending the night bathing, turning, and helping feed my dad. I was grateful that my job allowed me to do this and can look back and appreciate that time I had with family. October 27  was the day that things took a turn. Daddy complained of chest pain and shortness of breath, so my sister contacted 911, the EMT took him to the ER. Labs and all other tests were okay so doctors decided to keep my dad to treat his dialysis while there. He developed complications while on dialysis, and that is when we decided that his body just could not take it anymore.

That day my dad came back home to be on hospice care. Daddy told everyone that he loved us. Those next few days were the toughest days of my life. Watching my dad slowly transition has been the hardest thing that I had to deal with in my life. I had to learn to separate myself from being the nurse to being the daughter. My mom, sisters, and I wanted to make sure that Daddy was comfortable, cared for, loved, and did not have any pain. I remember a couple of days before he went home to be with the Lord, my dad grabbed my shirt and said, "You know I love you." And I told him that I loved him too. The next day he stopped talking.

Tuesday, November 3, 2020, is a day that I will always remember. My mom, sisters, and I would tag team to get my dad bathed and dressed. That morning my mom woke up and said that my dad was just there, no movement. He was breathing but not moaning as we moved him. I had a feeling that this would be the day that God would call my dad home. I decided to call two of my sisters that were not there; once they were on the phone, my two sisters that were there, and my mother prayed around my dad. We prayed for a peaceful transition. As the day went by, a couple of family members stopped by, my sisters and I would turn him periodically, kiss him, rub his shoulders, and provide pain medication to help him relax. I can remember the hospice nurse coming by in the morning, she took one look at Daddy, and her disposition changed. When she walked outside, she turned around, looked at me, and said: "I'm sorry." My wish was that when my dad took his final breath, it would only be with my siblings and my mom. As the day continued, my dad began to develop fevers; I would give him a Tylenol suppository to control his temperature so that he could be comfortable. Then the evening occurred, it was about 7:42 pm when my mom was cleaning his colostomy bag, my sister gave my dad some liquid Ativan (medication used to help relax), and we turned him. At this very moment, I believe in my heart that God was leading me to speak to him. I told my dad that:

Me: *This battle is no longer yours; it's the Lords. You fought a good fight; you are a true soldier. We are proud of you. We know that you love us, and we love you too. God is looking down and saying, well done thy good and faithful servant. And don't worry, Mommy will remain the captain and boss someone else around. I love you, daddy.*

Sister: *I love you, daddy.*

Sister: *I love you, daddy.*

Mommy: *I love you, Wayne; you can go.*

Daddy opened up one eye at that very moment, then both eyes looked up to the heavens and took one final breath. Just then, he had transitioned. We then bathed my dad, dressed him in some new pajamas, and applied his favorite cologne- Royal Copenhagen. Afterward, we contacted some family members and the hospice agency, and a nurse came to pronounce my dad, which is when we had a close-out prayer with my family surrounding my daddy. I thanked God for a peaceful transition. Lastly, the undertaker came and draped his body bag with the American flag. It gives me peace knowing that Daddy's transition was one of peace till the very end. And that is what we prayed for that morning- God's peace.

I would have never imagined that this would have occurred so soon. I mean, my Dad has been a fighter. Placed on a ventilator multiple times, coded several times, and beat the odds even when the physicians thought he would not make it. That is because God is the great physician. He knows the day, hour, and minute. While we did not talk much about sickness, when I look back, I think my dad knew it was coming near, that God would call him home soon. Weeks before his transition, he told different people that he loved them and appreciated their friendship. I believe that God was trying to prepare me too. I was just in denial. I can remember one car ride heading to Raul's Barber Shop he told me that he might not decide on chemotherapy. He thought that his body could not tolerate it. I was beginning to accept God's plan for him. I believe that Daddy was accepting God's plan as well.

As I think about my Dad's transition, I think about his life, the life he lived, the love he gave, and the lives that he touched. Although Daddy is no longer here on earth, his presence and love remain present. And I am holding on to those memories, his many sayings, and all the fun times we shared. He was and continues to be my *hero, soldier*, and *Daddy*.

Reflection: Looking back at my Dad's final moments, I think about how my family came together in unity. We put our differences aside and thought about what was best for Daddy and at the same time took care of my mom and tried meeting her needs. Honestly, this time of transition has been tough, rough, and at times my heart does ache. During this time of transitioning, it has been a time of transformation. And I continue to be transformed.

Call for Action: Are you holding on to something that you should let go of?

Reflections

"My mission in life is not merely to survive, but to thrive; and to do so with some passion, some compassion, some humor, and some style."
Maya Angelou

When I reflect on the phases of my life, the woman that I have become, and my dad's journey, there are many lessons that I have learned, battles that were won. Despite the illnesses, challenges that my dad faced, he lived his life to the fullest. He appreciated the simple things in life such as fishing, playing chess, watching sports on television, and cruising. Daddy helped other veterans in making sure that they received their benefits; he was a proud Vietnam War Veteran. I reflect on the words he told me one car ride. He said: *"Yogi, I just want you to be happy."* Wow. Happy - What makes me happy? For a long time, I consumed myself with my job, my professional growth. While I took time throughout the years making sure my family was ok, attending doctor's appointments for my dad, and maintained being an advocate for both my parents. Work symbolized a getaway for me. When I worked, I did not seem to think about anything else. Now is that time to think about not only what makes me happy but also what fills my heart with joy. Because happiness is temporary -joy is everlasting. I am ready to embark on the next chapter of my life.

When my father transitioned, I felt a sense of emptiness, and at times I still do. I thought to myself, what do I do now? My dad was my biggest cheerleader and a great secret holder (lolol!). If you told him something in secrecy, he would not tell a soul! I no longer have my daddy-daughter rides anymore. When I accomplished something, daddy would be one of the first people that I told. Even though he may not have understood everything or what it all meant, he was proud. So, where do I go from here? When life happens, it makes you take a step back to reflect on things.

One day I was listening to a video, and the person spoke about peace. They stated that you should make peace with your past so that it would not interrupt your present. Make peace with my past? What does that mean to you? For me, that means working on my relationship with my mother and talking more, spending time together, and getting to know one another. It means making peace with the past hurts even when I did not receive an apology. It also means forgiving myself, letting go, and letting God.

I questioned if I was living my full purpose and being intentional with every aspect of my life. Sometimes I tend to do things without even thinking about time, the purpose, advantages, and disadvantages. I never wanted to say no in my past even if that meant that I was overwhelmed, overworked, and stressed out. For a long time, I put my wants, my needs, and my desires at the bottom of the list. But guess what? Not anymore! I learned that if someone asks me to do something, I do not have to respond immediately.

During this time of reflection, I learned the importance of speaking over myself - Positive affirmations. Some of the things that I speak over myself are: *"I am more than a conqueror," "All things are possible." I am beautiful", 'I am a Queen", I am valuable." "I deserve love," "I am loved," and "I am bold, strong, and resilient,"* At times I believe that others may think that I have it all together because I have the career and the degrees. But that does not make the person. I have my good days and bad days. Sometimes I have my sad days, and I ask God when it will be my time, my turn for certain things to occur in my life. I know that I am under construction and a work in progress. And in due season, I will have the desires of my heart.

So what does this next chapter look like for

Yolanda "Dr. Y"? I believe this next phase of my life is going to be filled with *self-care, love, discovery, family unity, travel, and taking leaps of faith.*

Self-care- I am set to take care of my mental, emotional, spiritual, and physical health.

Love- I am ready to share my life with whom God has destined for me.

Discovery- Time to embark on some new ventures, walk in my purpose and expand my territory.

Family unity- During this transition, I learned to put my differences aside, pray more, and communicate. I also am learning that every interaction does not require a reaction.

Travel- Once I can, I want to continue traveling, enjoying the beach (I call it my Beach Chronicles), and taking road trips with friends and family.

Taking Leaps of Faith- I am learning that I am bold, strong, fearless, and confident in my abilities. I can do all things through Christ that strengthens me Philippians 4:13. In this next chapter of my life, I will walk in boldness. When I am fearful, I will speak to myself. When

I am anxious, I will think about my natural father, daddy (now my guardian angel), and my spiritual father- God. You know my favorite saying is: *You got to name it, claim it, believe it, receive it, and then walk in it.* With that being said, I am going to practice what I preach!!

You know, when I considered the title of this book: *Daddy's Girl- A Daughter's Tribute*, I think about living life to the fullest. That is what my dad would have wanted. So as I take on this next chapter of my life, I will hold on to my dad's memories, I know that his presence and love will forever remain with me. I can still hear his voice, the smell his cologne, and hear his laughter. Thankful for every experience. The bond we shared was one that I will always cherish. Although he is no longer here on earth, he is now my guardian angel. I know as time goes, I will have moments of sadness, joy, and uncertainty. But with God on my side, I will make it through, and so can you!

I don't know what the future holds, but I am excited to take the ride! And as I take on this next chapter, I will always think of you Daddy and make you proud!

Sincerely,
Daddy's Girl

Reflection: As I reflect on this journey of writing this memoir, I know that my life matters. God loves me and says that I am fearfully and wonderfully made. Daddy made sure that I knew that by his way of support and love. And I will forever be grateful for that. At the same time that I know that my heavenly Father and natural father have encouraged me, I also have to encourage and motivate myself.

Call for Action: As you reflect on your life, are there ways to empower yourself and others that are currently missing?

Daddy's Girl

A Daughter's Tribute

Today my spirit is conflicted, I'm sad yet I'm glad,
Not everyone had the luxury of a nurturing, loving Dad.
But in Wayne F. Nelson – this is what I had.

From childhood to the present, you supplied my every need,
Then equipped me to go confidently, in the world and succeed.

As life progressed, I realized time spent with you was a treasure,
Weekly barbershop trips became my anticipated pleasure.

Your nuggets of wisdom, your humor, your favorite saying,
Remain a loop in my heart, continuously playing.

"You gotta hook 'em to cook 'em" will forever bring a smile,
Your patience, while fishing…that was your style.

Sports enthusiast and master of chess,
Listening to jazz was all a part of your finesse.

You were a tough Marine and Veteran Purple Heart,
Your cancer diagnosis was just another battle fought.

And with the grace of God and His permission,
You beat your cancer back into remission.

God knew you weren't done watching the "Bold and Beautiful"
And that your work with the VFW was necessary and dutiful.

He knew we weren't ready for you to depart,
So He took control of your medical charts,
To give us more time to prepare our hearts.

Alas your purpose on earth had been fulfilled,
Leaving a foundation of love on which to build.

It gives me comfort knowing that this departure isn't the end,
And that, in time, we will reunite again.

So I'll reflect on your memories, knowing you're watching over
me,
I'll rejoice in the knowledge that you are pain free.

And we know the prayers of a righteous man are effectual and
fervent,
Hence my last words to you Dad: "God is looking down saying;
Well done, thy good and faithful servant."

Poem written by Toni Jacobe

Call for Action Reflections:
Take a moment to consider the contents of the
chapters, what resonated with you?

Call for Action #1: Think about a young memory of
your life. What if you could talk to your teenage self,
the one thing you would say would be?

_____

_____

_____

_____

_____

_____

_____

_____

_____

_____

_____

_____

_____

Call for Action #2:
Questions to consider:
1. What motivates you?
2. How are you showing up in the world?
3. What keeps you grounded?

_____

_____

_____

_____

_____

_____

_____

_____

_____

_____

_____

_____

_____

Call for Action #3:

What are you doing about the things that matter most in your life? If you had no limits or fears, what do you want to give yourself permission to do, discover, or make room for this year?

_____

_____

_____

_____

_____

_____

_____

_____

_____

_____

_____

_____

_____

_____

Call for Action #4:

While you are making plans keep in mind to set goals, there are decisions that you will also have to make. Decisions can be simple or complicated. Considering your personal and/or professional journey, what decisions do you need to make currently? Have you taken time to reflect?

_____

_____

_____

_____

_____

_____

_____

_____

_____

_____

_____

_____

Call for Action #5:

Are you holding on to something that you should let go of?

_____

_____

_____

_____

_____

_____

_____

_____

_____

_____

_____

_____

_____

_____

Call for Action #6:

As you reflect on your life, are there ways to empower yourself and others that are currently missing?

_____

_____

_____

_____

_____

_____

_____

_____

_____

_____

_____

_____

_____

About the Author

Yolanda Nelson is a woman on the move, currently under construction, and determined to make an impact on this world.

As a daughter, aunt, mentor, friend, nursing professor, and author, Yolanda takes advantage of every opportunity to help others discover their passions in life. She understands the value of self-reflection and the importance of planting seeds in others. Her saying is that "I assist in planting the seed and it is the person's job to cultivate it".

Another desire of Yolanda's is to increase the diversity within the profession of nursing. Her mission has been mentoring students of color. To build upon their self-confidence, leadership skills, and critical thinking. As a result of mentoring nursing students, students have been granted opportunities for scholarships, research projects, publications, and speaking engagements. Yolanda currently leads 3 mentorship programs that are thriving.

As Yolanda has been soaring professionally in her career as Nurse Educator, Mentor, Author, and Entrepreneur, she understands the significance of self-care, loving yourself, and the importance of saying **No**. She is on a mission to living a more fulfilled life.

Memories help to mold us into who we are. Yolanda is a true testament that you can be resilient despite your life's circumstances and make a difference in this world.